40

Famous

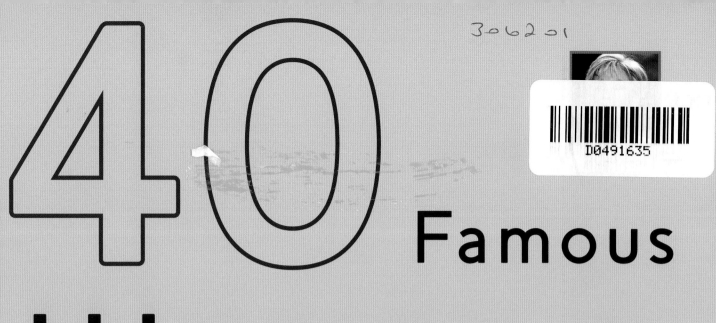

Women

By Diane Hoyt-Goldsmith

Series Literacy Consultant
Dr Ros Fisher

Pearson Education Limited
Edinburgh Gate
Harlow
Essex CM20 2JE
England

www.longman.co.uk

ISBN 0 582 84136 4

Colour reproduction by Colourscan, Singapore
Printed and bound in China by Leo Paper Products Ltd.

The Publisher's policy is to use paper manufactured from sustainable forests.

The following people from **DK** have
contributed to the development of this product:

Art Director Rachael Foster

Martin Wilson **Managing Art Editor** | **Managing Editor** Marie Greenwood
Nicola Liddiard, Jane Tetzlaff **Design** | **Editorial** Selina Wood
Marie Ortu, Pernilla Pearce **Picture Research** | **Production** Gordana Simakovic
Richard Czapnik, Andy Smith **Cover Design** | **DTP** David McDonald
Consultant Philip Wilkinson

Dorling Kindersley would like to thank: Peter Dennis and Tony Walter-Bellue for original artwork;
Johnny Pau for additional cover design work.

Introduction

Women have contributed to the world and its cultures in many ways. Women are heads of state, scientists and athletes. They are writers, astronauts and teachers. They are explorers, artists and crusaders for social change. So many women have accomplished so many important achievements that no book could include them all. This book gives information about some of the amazing women who have contributed so much to the world.

Many of the women in this book are still living today. You might read about them in tomorrow's newspaper, hear about them on the radio or see them on television. They continue to make important contributions, some of which may affect your life.

Icon Key
Each woman falls into one of five categories. Each category is represented by a coloured icon, which appears next to the entry.

Arts

History

Science & Exploration

Sports

World Leader

Isabel Allende

Isabel Allende 1942–

Writer, CHILE

Isabel Allende was born in Lima, Peru. She and her family moved to Chile when she was three. She grew up surrounded by talented and highly educated people. She was the niece and goddaughter of Chile's president, Salvador Allende. Allende was working as a journalist when her uncle was assassinated in 1973. This forced her to move to Venezuela with her husband and children. Today, she lives in the United States.

Allende's first book, *The House of the Spirits*, grew out of letters she wrote to her family in Chile. It tells the history of Chile through strong female characters who survive political violence. Publishers in her own country refused to publish the book. However, the book was published in Spain in 1982. It was translated into many languages, including English. Several more successful books followed.

Allende says her most personal book was written for her daughter, Paula Frias, who died in 1992. Money from the book's sales goes to the Isabel Allende Foundation. The Foundation honours and continues Paula's work with poor communities, especially women and children.

Allende at a book signing in 1993

Maria Corazon Aquino 1933–

President, PHILIPPINES

Maria Corazon Aquino, known as Cory, was born in Manila, in the Philippines. She went to college in the United States. Then she returned to the Philippines in 1953 to go to law school. In 1954 she married Benigno Aquino, the youngest senator ever elected in the Philippines. Because they opposed dictator Ferdinand Marcos, the Aquinos were forced to leave the Philippines in 1972. On their return in 1983, Marcos's soldiers assassinated Benigno Aquino. Unafraid, Cory Aquino ran for president against Marcos in 1986. During the election, Marcos's many illegal activities were revealed. He was forced to leave the country. Aquino became the Philippines' first female president. In office, Aquino set political prisoners free and reinstated a democratically elected Congress.

Maria Corazon Aquino

Three million Filipinos attended a thanksgiving mass for Aquino's new government on 2nd March, 1986. Aquino remained president until 1992.

Margaret Bourke-White

Margaret Bourke-White 1906–1971

Photojournalist, UNITED STATES

Margaret Bourke-White, born in New York City, New York, became the first woman to work in the field of photojournalism – telling a news story through photographs. She first specialized in industrial photography. She took dramatic shots of factories, businesses and architecture. In 1935 the brand-new magazine *Life* employed Bourke-White. One of her photographs was on the magazine's first front cover. During World War II, she was the first female war reporter to go to Europe. She survived a torpedo blast and flew on combat missions. In later years, Bourke-White's profession took her all over the world. She captured images that were both beautiful and informative for magazine readers of all ages.

Bourke-White perched on a gargoyle on the Chrysler Building to photograph the Manhattan skyline.

Ada Byron (Lady Lovelace) 1815–1852

Mathematician, UNITED KINGDOM

Born in London, Ada Byron was the daughter of Lord Byron, a famous poet. She, however, studied to become a scientist and mathematician. She brought imagination and creativity to mathematics. In 1834 Byron translated into English an Italian article about Charles Babbage, the inventor of an imaginary calculating machine. This machine would both make predictions and act on them. Byron added her own ideas to Babbage's theory. Her plan is now regarded as the very first computer programme.

Ada Byron, Lady Lovelace

Maria Cristina Caballero 1963–

Journalist, COLOMBIA

Maria Cristina Caballero's journalism career began when she was sixteen. While attending Javeriana University in Bogotá, Colombia, in South America, Caballero wrote for the newspapers *La Republica* and *El Tiempo* – Colombia's leading daily paper. After graduating, Caballero became a respected journalist who risked her life to investigate the violence and human rights abuses in her country. Her interviews with leaders on both sides of the conflict resulted in *Peace on the Table*. This document offered solutions to her country's problems. She has won several awards, including the Simón Bolívar National Prize for Journalism, the Inter-American Press Association's Human Rights Journalism Award and the New York–based Committee to Protect Journalists' World Press Freedom Award. Today, Caballero is a fellow at Harvard University's Center for Public Leadership.

Maria Cristina Caballero

Helen Caldicott

 # Helen Caldicott 1938–

Physician and Peace Advocate, AUSTRALIA

Helen Caldicott is one of the world's leading anti-nuclear activists. She was born in Melbourne, Australia, and graduated from medical school at the University of Adelaide. In the 1970s radioactive fallout from French nuclear tests in the Pacific was affecting the air and water quality of some places in Australia. Beginning in 1971, Caldicott played a major role in leading Australia's opposition to the French nuclear tests.

Between 1977 and 1986 Dr Caldicott practised medicine in the United States. There, she organized Physicians for Social Responsibility. This group of more than 20,000 doctors educates the public about the dangers of nuclear weapons and nuclear war. Caldicott also founded Women's Action for Nuclear Disarmament (WAND). Two of Caldicott's well-known books are *Nuclear Madness* (1979) and *If You Love This Planet: A Plan to Heal the Earth* (1992).

Nuclear testing in Mururoa, French Polynesia, on October 1, 1977

Emily Carr 1872–1945

Author and Artist, CANADA

Emily Carr was born in Victoria, Vancouver Island. She enjoyed art from when she was a young child. She began her formal training at the California School of Design, in San Francisco, in 1890. In 1899 she went to England to study painting. When she arrived back home, Carr saw the totem poles of Canada's native people for the first time. The young artist was so impressed by these sculptures that she decided to make paintings of all the totem poles in British Columbia. For the next four years, she worked on this project. She created more than 200 images. The paintings were displayed in an exhibition called Canadian West Coast Art – Native and Modern. By the time she died in 1945, she had written and published a number of books about her life and work.

Emily Carr

Caroline Chisholm 1808–1877

Social Worker and Reformer, AUSTRALIA

Caroline Chisholm

Born in England, Caroline Chisholm left her home in Northampton in 1838 to emigrate to Australia. At that time, there were many convicts from England and Ireland imprisoned in Sydney. Chisholm was disturbed that the wives of some of the convicts, their children and single women immigrants were often homeless. She set up a home where these women and children could live while they looked for employment. It was known as the Female Immigrant's Home, and provided assistance for more than a thousand women. In 1846 Chisholm returned to England to persuade the government to help other families move to Australia to find a better life.

Bessie Coleman

 # Bessie Coleman 1892–1926

Aviator, UNITED STATES

Born in Texas, Bessie Coleman moved to Chicago, Illinois, in 1915 to work as a beautician. Coleman was fascinated by aeroplanes, and dreamed of becoming a pilot. At the time, however, both gender and racial discrimination in the United States made it impossible for her to learn to fly. Still, she refused to give up her dream.

In 1920 Coleman travelled to France. There, she attended flight school and earned a pilot's licence. Back home, no American companies would employ an African-American woman pilot. So, Coleman decided to learn acrobatic flying. In the early 1920s air shows were popular. Pilots called "barnstormers" entertained crowds with daring tricks. Between 1921 and 1925 Coleman appeared in many air shows. She gained a reputation for her thrilling stunts. In 1926 Coleman's career came to a tragic end when she fell from her plane and died.

Coleman, at twenty-four, receiving a bouquet from Captain Edison C McVey, aeronautical instructor of United Airlines

Marie Curie 1867–1934

Physicist and Chemist, FRANCE

Born Marya Sklodowska in Warsaw, Poland, Marie Curie became the first woman to receive two Nobel Prizes: one in physics and one in chemistry. She was educated at the Sorbonne in Paris. There, she met her future husband, Pierre Curie. The Curies worked side by side on many research projects. One of their interests was radioactivity. Together they discovered two new chemical elements and performed numerous experiments.

After Pierre died, Marie and her daughter, Irene, continued working with radiation in the form of X-rays. At that time, scientists had not yet learned of the dangers of exposure to radiation. After years of experiments with radioactivity, Marie Curie became ill and died from leukaemia.

Marie Curie in her Paris laboratory

Catriona LeMay Doan 1970–

Speed Skater, CANADA

Catriona LeMay Doan was the world's fastest woman on ice. She won a gold medal in the 500-metre skating event in the 1998 Olympics in Nagano, Japan. She won this race in an Olympic record time. Born in Saskatoon, Saskatchewan, she started competing in speed skating in 1985. In 1998, 2001 and 2002 she was named Canada's Female Athlete of the Year. At the 2000–2001 Canadian National Championships, Doan shattered the world record set in 1997 with a time of 37.40 seconds for the 500-metre race. After twenty-three years of skating, Doan retired from the Canadian National Speed Skating Team in May 2003.

Catriona LeMay Doan on her way to a gold medal at the 1998 Winter Olympics

Gloria Estefan 1957–

Singer, UNITED STATES

Not long after Gloria Maria Fajardo was born in Havana, Cuba, her family fled to Miami, Florida, during the Cuban Revolution. As a young child, Estefan sang Cuban songs to the many women whose husbands were fighting in the war. Singing music from her homeland was one way she connected with her lost Cuba.

In the 1980s Estefan was the lead singer for a band called Miami Sound Machine. She and her husband, Emilio, made Latin rhythms part of mainstream pop music. Since then, Estefan has drawn from her success to make a difference in society. In 1990 Gloria met US President George Bush to discuss her participation in an anti-drugs programme. Shortly after this meeting, she was seriously injured in a bus accident. Estefan never gave up her determination to recover. In less than a year, she was performing on stage again.

After Hurricane Andrew swept through Florida in 1992, Estefan wrote a song, titled "Always Tomorrow", for the hurricane victims. She later organized a relief concert. The money earned from both the song and the concert was donated to aid the hurricane victims. Estefan is a talented entertainer who has made great contributions to society. She continues to speak out on behalf of freedom for fellow Cubans.

Gloria Estefan

Eka Esu-Williams 1950–

Scientist and Health Worker, NIGERIA

Eka Esu-Williams was born in northern Nigeria.
After studying biology at the University of Nigeria,
she moved to London. She worked for her graduate
degree in immunology at the University of London.
Immunology is the study of how the body resists diseases.

Esu-Williams returned to Nigeria in 1985 and worked
in the fight against AIDS – Acquired Immune Deficiency
Syndrome. This disease was spreading rapidly among
African women in the mid-1980s. A lack of information
contributed to the spread of AIDS. In 1988
Esu-Williams founded the Society of Women
Against AIDS. The Society educates women
on how to avoid AIDS. It has branches
in twenty-nine African countries.
It also works closely with other health
organizations to encourage national
governments to help prevent the
spread of AIDS.

Eka Esu-Williams

Esu-Williams with
children and staff
from a day-care
centre supported
by the Society
of Women
Against AIDS

Catherine Freeman 1973–

Runner, AUSTRALIA

Catherine Freeman

Cathy Freeman ran her first race when she was eight years old. She won her first gold medal at the Commonwealth Games at the age of sixteen in 1990. In that same year, she was awarded the title of Young Australian of the Year. Then in 1991 she was named Aboriginal Athlete of the Year. In the following year, Freeman travelled to Barcelona, Spain. There, she became the first Aboriginal track athlete to represent Australia in the Olympic Games.

In 1998 she was awarded one of the greatest honours in Australia when she was named Australian of the Year.

During the 2000 Olympics in Sydney, Freeman was given the honour of lighting the Olympic flame at the opening cermony. She went on to win a gold medal in the 400-metre race. After carrying both the Australian and Aboriginal flags around the track, she said "I just want to show I am proud of who I am and where I come from." She retired from racing in July 2003.

Catherine Freeman, right, winning the Women's 400-metre final at the 2000 Olympic Games in Sydney

Birute Galdikas 1946–

Anthropologist, INDONESIA

Birute Galdikas

Canadian Birute Galdikas was born in Germany while her parents were travelling from Lithuania to Canada. Since the 1980s, she has been studying orangutans in the swamps and jungles of Borneo, in Asia. Galdikas is studying these endangered animals because she believes that learning about orangutans' behaviour can help scientists learn more about humans. She is an Indonesian citizen and spends at least half of each year in Borneo. In addition to her award-winning work in animal science, Galdikas speaks out for the preservation and conservation of habitats where orangutans and other wild species live.

Indira Gandhi 1917–1984

Prime Minister, INDIA

The only child of Jawaharlal Nehru, India's first prime minister, Indira Gandhi grew up among politicians. During India's struggle for independence from Great Britain, her parents were often imprisoned for their political activities. In 1959 she was selected as president of the Indian National Congress Party, the second highest political position in India. In 1967 Gandhi was elected as India's first woman prime minister and the leader of the world's largest democracy. She lost her position as prime minister in 1977. However, she was re-elected in 1980. Gandhi raised India's standard of living. She also excelled in foreign policy, leading a victory over Pakistan in 1971. She was assassinated in 1984.

Indira Gandhi

Tanni Grey-Thompson 1969–

Wheelchair Athlete, UNITED KINGDOM

Tanni Grey-Thompson
at the Paralympic
Games in 1996

Tanni Grey-Thompson was born in Cardiff, Wales, with a disease called spina bifida. She was confined to a wheelchair from the age of eight. She never wanted to let her disability prevent her from participating in sports. At the age of thirteen, Grey-Thompson began to race in her wheelchair. In 1992 she won her first Paralympic gold medal in Barcelona, Spain. By 2000, at the end of the Sydney Games, she had won nine gold medals. Grey-Thompson has received many awards including Member of the British Empire (MBE) in 1992 for her services to people in sports with disabilities. She was named Welsh Woman of the Year in 2001. She is also one of forty-two members of the World Sports Academy.

Sachiko Hashimoto 1909–1995

Red Cross Leader, JAPAN

Sachiko Hashimoto

Sachiko Hashimoto graduated from Japan's Women's University in 1930 with a degree in English. After the surrender of Japan in World War II, Hashimoto worked to rebuild the Japanese Red Cross Society. By that time, the Japanese Red Cross had been in existence for almost seventy years. She was in charge of reforming the Junior Red Cross in Japan. She devoted her life to training young volunteers. In 1972 she was the first Asian woman to be awarded the Henry Dunant Medal for her hard work and dedication in youth education.

Frida Kahlo 1907–1954

Artist, MEXICO

Frida Kahlo was badly injured in an accident when she was fifteen. She began to paint during her long recovery period. This led to her becoming a successful painter, even though she was ill and in pain most of her life. Her husband, Diego Rivera, was also a great painter. He once said of her work, "She is the only woman to express in her work an art of the feelings, functions and the creative power of woman."

Frida Kahlo

Helen Keller 1880–1968

Writer and Teacher, UNITED STATES

Keller, left, with Anne Sullivan

When Helen Keller was a baby in Alabama, she had an illness that left her blind and deaf. Despite these disabilities, she achieved a number of important goals. When Keller was six, Anne Sullivan became her teacher. She taught Keller to use her sense of touch to learn the alphabet and braille. She also taught her how to speak.

Eventually, Keller graduated from college with honours. She went to work as a teacher for the American Foundation for the Blind. Later, she continued her work with people who were deaf and blind by starting the Helen Keller Endowment Fund. Keller's speeches and writings such as *The Story of My Life* and *The World I Live In*, made her famous.

Aung San Suu Kyi 1945–

Peace Activist, MYANMAR

Aung San Suu Kyi

Aung San Suu Kyi grew up in a political family. Her father, General Aung San, led the country when it gained independence from Great Britain in 1947. Her mother, Daw Khin Kyi, was the Burmese representative to India and Nepal.

Aung San Suu Kyi was educated in India and England, where she attended Oxford University. She entered politics in 1988 when she returned to Burma to care for her mother. At that time, demonstrations for change led to violence. As a result, many people were hurt. Aung San Suu Kyi believed that violence would not help her country and its people. She became the leader of the political party called the National League for Democracy. She worked hard to convince others that they needed to work towards democracy. Aung San Suu Kyi was offered the opportunity to leave the country. However, she knew that if she did, she would not be allowed to return. She decided to stay. In 1991 Aung San Suu Kyi was awarded the Nobel Peace Prize. Her eldest son, Alexander Aris, accepted the award on behalf of his mother.

Aung San Suu Kyi at a press conference in 1995 after her release following six years of house arrest

Maya Lin 1959–

Architect, UNITED STATES

Maya Lin

Maya Lin was born and raised in Athens, Ohio. While studying architecture at Yale University, Lin entered a competition to design the Vietnam Veterans Memorial in Washington, DC. She was only twenty-one years old when her design was chosen from about 1,400 entries.

Lin's monument is a simple wall of black marble that rises from the earth. The names of all the soldiers who were lost in combat are engraved in rows on the shiny black stone. She has also designed a civil rights memorial in Alabama and numerous buildings. Lin's wide-ranging interests include Japanese gardens and Native American earthworks.

The Vietnam Veterans Memorial in Washington, DC, United States

Wangari Maathai

Wangari Maathai 1940–

Environmentalist, KENYA

Born in Nyeri, Kenya, Wangari Maathai travelled to the United States to attend college. When she returned to Kenya, she studied at the University of Nairobi. Maathai became the first woman in central and eastern Africa to earn a Ph.D.

Maathai was focusing on the lives of poor women and Kenya's environment in the 1970s when she started a work programme to plant trees. At the time, Kenya was suffering from severe deforestation. Few trees were planted to replace those cut down for firewood. In 2003 Maathai became the deputy minister in the Ministry of Environment, Natural Resources and Wildlife.

Moscoso in 1999, after meeting with US President Bill Clinton

Mireya Elisa Moscoso 1946–

President, PANAMA

Mireya Elisa Moscoso grew up in a poor family in Panama City. After leaving school, she went to work as a secretary. In 1968 Moscoso married the former president of Panama, Arnulfo Arias.

After his death in 1988, Moscoso helped create a new political party in Panama – the Arnulfista. As leader of this party, she ran for president of Panama in 1994 and again in 1999. Her 1999 campaign which called for more jobs and better schools, was successful. She became Panama's first woman president. During her presidency, the United States returned control of the Panama Canal to Panama. Mireya Moscoso then worked to make the canal a profitable business zone.

Florence Nightingale 1820–1910

Nurse and Educator, UNITED KINGDOM

Born in Florence, Italy, Florence Nightingale trained as a nurse in Europe. Later, she became the supervisor of a women's hospital in London. When the Crimean War began in Russia in 1854, Nightingale volunteered for duty.

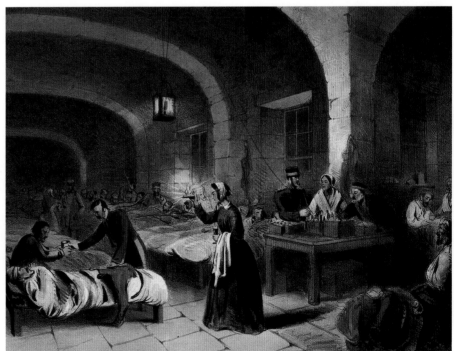

Florence Nightingale

At that time, nursing was not the respected profession that it is today. Also, most hospitals were very unclean. This changed partly as a result of Nightingale's work. She took thirty-eight nurses with her and set up a hospital near the battle lines. There, her modern nursing methods greatly reduced the number of deaths from infection.

After the war ended, the British government gave Nightingale funds to set up and run a training programme for nurses. She was awarded many honours. In 1907 she became the first woman to receive the British Order of Merit from King Edward VII.

These paintings show hospital conditions before and after Nightingale's work.

Antonia Novello 1944–

Surgeon General and Advocate for Children, UNITED STATES

Antonia Novello

Antonia Novello was born in Fajardo, Puerto Rico. Novello had some serious health problems as a child. This led to her decision to become a pediatrician. After college, Novello attended the University of Puerto Rico Medical School. She worked as an intern at the University of Michigan Medical Center. Later, she joined the National Institute of Health (NIH). There, her area of special interest was children with AIDS.

Novello's work with children led US President George HW Bush to appoint her surgeon general in 1990. The surgeon general is the chief medical officer of the US government's health services. As surgeon general, Novello helped improve and expand health services for children. Later, she worked for children's health and nutrition at the United Nations Children's Fund (UNICEF). In 1999 she became commissioner of health for the State of New York.

Antonia Novello, as surgeon general, promoting vaccinations in a Children's Health Fund mobile medical unit in 1991

Ellen Ochoa 1958–

Astronaut, UNITED STATES

Ellen Ochoa was the first Hispanic-American woman in space. Ochoa was born in Los Angeles, California, to parents who were immigrants from Mexico. She studied physics at San Diego State University and graduated at the top of her class. Later, she received a master's degree and a PhD in electrical engineering from Stanford University. In the mid-1980s Ochoa worked as a research engineer. In 1990 NASA (National Aeronautics and Space Administration) chose her to train as an astronaut at the Johnson Space Center. Three years later, Ochoa was part of a team on the space shuttle *Discovery* to study Earth's ozone layer. Since then, she has flown several missions. Often her job has been to control the space shuttle's robotic arm during work outside the shuttle.

Ellen Ochoa playing the flute for her fellow crew members while on a space mission in April 1993

Patricia O'Shane 1941–

Magistrate, AUSTRALIA

Patricia O'Shane was born and raised in the small sugar-producing town of Mosman, Queensland. She is of mixed Irish and Aboriginal heritage. After receiving a degree in education, O'Shane became a teacher. Later, she went back to school to earn a law degree. As a lawyer, Pat O'Shane fought to improve the health, housing and education of her people – the Aboriginal people of Australia. In 1981 O'Shane was named head of the Department of Aboriginal Affairs in New South Wales. In 1986 she became the first Aboriginal judge in Sydney's court system. She continues to be an advocate for the rights of all people.

Pat O'Shane speaking at the Step To The Future Youth Leadership Forum in 2003

Rosa Parks receiving the
Congressional Gold Medal on
15th June, 1999

Rosa Parks 1913–

Civil Rights Heroine, UNITED STATES

Rosa Parks knew what it was like to have no civil rights. She grew up in the segregated southern United States. As an adult, she worked with her husband to help improve the lives of African-Americans. One evening in 1955, she boarded a bus in Montgomery, Alabama. As the bus became crowded, the driver told Parks to give up her seat for a white person. She refused and was arrested.

Parks's actions sparked a bus boycott, led by Dr Martin Luther King Jr, in Montgomery. For over a year, African Americans refused to ride the city buses. The US Supreme Court later ruled that segregation, the separation of people based on race, on buses was illegal. As a result, the boycott finally ended.

This ruling brought changes all over the country. It also helped end segregation in the South. For her role in advancing civil rights, Parks received the Presidential Medal of Freedom in 1996 and the Congressional Gold Medal in 1999.

Parks refused to give up her
seat on a crowded bus in
Alabama in 1955.

Mary West Pratt 1935–

Artist, CANADA

Canadian painter Mary West Pratt was born in Fredericton, New Brunswick. Since 1961 she has lived and painted in Newfoundland. When Pratt was only eleven, one of her paintings was selected for an international exhibition. This experience convinced her to pursue a career in painting. While studying fine art, she met her husband Christopher Pratt. She encouraged him to take up painting as a career. Ironically, his career blossomed while she took several years off to raise their family. Then Pratt began a series of small paintings of various household items. In her paintings, she focused on the play of light on these objects.

In the 1970s Pratt began to achieve success as a result of a number of local and international exhibitions of her paintings. She continues to paint and display her work. She also takes a very active role in Canadian cultural affairs. In 1997 she was honoured as a Companion of the Order of Canada.

Mary West Pratt

Left: *Supper Table*, painted in 1969

Below: *Eggs in Egg Crate*, painted in 1975

Mary Robinson 1944–

President and Human Rights Activist, IRELAND

Robinson meeting young children at an educational programme centre on the outskirts of Bangkok, Thailand, on 1st March, 2001

Mary Robinson was educated at Trinity College in Dublin. She went on to earn a master of law degree at Harvard University, in the United States. She was a member of Ireland's Senate between 1969 and 1989 and professor of law at Trinity College. In December 1990 Robinson was elected as Ireland's first woman president.

President Robinson used her power to draw attention to countries in Africa and Asia that faced famine, disease and genocide. Genocide is the widespread killing of specific groups of people for their race or beliefs. This work led to her being appointed as the United Nations High Commissioner for Human Rights. In that position, Robinson spoke out against abuses of human rights wherever they occurred.

Mary Grant Seacole 1805–1881

Nurse, UNITED KINGDOM

Mary Grant Seacole

Mary Grant Seacole was born in Kingston, Jamaica, where she trained to be a nurse. In 1854 she heard about the Crimean War (a war in which France and England fought against Russia). Seacole travelled to England, hoping to find work as a battlefield nurse. When racial prejudice prevented her from being employed as a nurse, Seacole went to the battlefield anyway. There, she set up a "British Hotel" and supplied hot meals while nursing the wounded soldiers. Later, British Queen Victoria honoured Mary Seacole for her bravery.

Laura Secord 1775–1868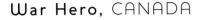

War Hero, CANADA

Laura Ingersoll was born in Great Barrington, Massachusetts, in the United States. After marrying James Secord, she moved to Queenston, Canada. At that time, Canada was a colony of Great Britain. During the War of 1812 between Great Britain and the United States, American soldiers invaded Canada. Secord's husband was wounded. Later, the Americans occupied her home. Forced to shelter and feed the soldiers, she learned of their plan to attack British and Canadian troops at Beaver Creek. Secord risked her life to warn the troops of this attack. As a result, the British and Canadian forces were able to surprise the Americans and win the battle. Years later in 1860, the Prince of Wales, a member of the British royal family, rewarded Secord for her bravery.

Laura Secord

Huda Shaarawi 1879–1947

Educator and Women's Rights Activist, EGYPT

Huda Shaarawi was born in Cairo, Egypt. At the age of thirteen, she was forced into an unhappy marriage. Shaarawi later worked to end rules and customs that were unfair to women. In 1910 Shaarawi opened a school for girls that taught academic subjects. Other girls' schools at that time taught homemaking skills only. Shaarawi also organized lectures for women. This brought many women out of their homes and into public places for the first time.

After her husband's death in 1923, Shaarawi stopped wearing her veil, or *hegab*. She was said to be the first woman in Cairo to break the tradition of covering the face in public.

Huda Shaarawi

Kate Sheppard

Kate Sheppard 1847–1934

Suffragist and Women's Rights Advocate, NEW ZEALAND

Catherine Wilson Malcolm was born in Liverpool, England, to Scottish parents. Although women did not have many opportunities at that time, she received a good education. In 1868 she and her family moved to New Zealand. There, she met Walter Allen Sheppard. They got married in 1871.

Sheppard was one of the leaders of the women's movement in New Zealand. In 1885 she was one of the founding members of the New Zealand Women's Christian Temperance Union. Sheppard strongly believed that women should have a greater role in society.

Sheppard supported the right of women to vote. She was a great leader in the long struggle to achieve women's suffrage in New Zealand. She prepared pamphlets and edited and wrote a women's page in the national temperance newspaper, *The Prohibitionist.*

Sheppard is seated fifth from the left in this 1896 photograph of the National Council of Women

Furthermore, she organized three successful petitions. The third petition was the largest one ever presented to Parliament. As a result, Parliament passed the Electoral Act in 1893. This act granted full voting rights to women. Sheppard is recognized as the key figure in the suffrage movement in New Zealand, the first country to grant voting rights to men and women equally.

Utako Shimodo c. 1854–c.1934

Educator and Women's Advocate, JAPAN

In mid-nineteenth-century Japan, girls did not go to school. Utako Shimodo's father was a scholar, however, and educated his daughter at home. As a young girl, she read all the books that were available to her. Later, Shimodo's father became an official for the Japanese emperor. This allowed Utako Shimodo to attend lectures by well-known scholars.

After her husband died, Shimodo devoted herself to women's education. She helped establish schools for girls and young women all over Japan. Shimodo encouraged the teaching of international perspectives in the new schools. She was also an advocate of scientific and medical research. Shimodo wrote eighty books on education, literature and other subjects.

Utako Shimodo

Kiri Te Kanawa in 2002, at a concert for the queen's golden jubilee

Kiri Te Kanawa 1944–

Opera Singer, NEW ZEALAND

Kiri Te Kanawa is Maori, the first people of New Zealand. Te Kanawa's international career began with her first appearance at the Royal Opera House in London. Her success as an opera singer seemed to come overnight after she sang the role of the Countess in *The Marriage of Figaro*.

In 1982 she was appointed a Dame Commander of the British Empire. This honorary title from the Queen recognizes her many contributions to music and opera. In 1999 Te Kanawa released an album of Maori songs, expressing her pride in her cultural background and helping to preserve it.

Valentina Tereshkova 1937–

Cosmonaut, RUSSIA

Valentina Tereshkova

Valentina Tereshkova was born to a peasant family in Masslennikovo in the Yaroslavl' region of the former Soviet Union, now part of Russia. In her late teens, she joined a club for amateur parachutists. In 1961 she applied to the Soviet space programme to become a cosmonaut. Tereshkova, three other women parachutists and a female aeroplane pilot were selected to train as cosmonauts in 1962. Tereshkova was the only one of the group to actually go into space. She became the first woman in space in 1963. At that time, the Soviet space programme was top secret. Tereshkova could not even tell her family that she was training to be a cosmonaut. Her mother only learned of her historic role in the Soviet space programme when the flight was announced on Radio Moscow shortly after take-off.

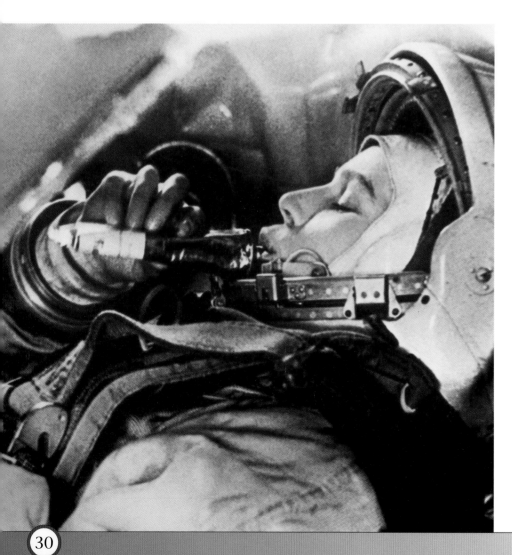

Tereshkova practised eating in flight simulations before going into space on 16th June, 1963.

Margaret Thatcher 1925–

Prime Minister, UNITED KINGDOM

Born Margaret Hilda Roberts in Grantham, Margaret Thatcher studied chemistry at Oxford University. She then studied law and was first elected to Parliament in 1959. In 1970 Thatcher became the first woman in Prime Minister Edward Heath's cabinet. At that time she served as the Minister for Education and Science. When Heath resigned from office in 1975, Thatcher became the leader of the Conservative Party. Four years later she became the first woman to be elected Prime Minister, breaking the 700-year-old tradition of rule by men. During her time in office Thatcher helped improve the United Kingdom's economy by making government and industry more efficient.

Margaret Thatcher

Harriet Tubman c. 1819–1913

American Abolitionist, UNITED STATES

Harriet Tubman was born into slavery and grew up on a plantation near Cambridge, Maryland, USA. At twenty-five, she fled north. During her escape, Tubman stayed in safe houses run by people who opposed slavery, a network called the Underground Railroad. After reaching freedom, Tubman herself became an active member of the Underground Railroad. She returned to the South at least eighteen times, and risked her life to help more than 300 slaves reach freedom in the North. During the Civil War (1861–1865) Tubman served as a spy, scout and nurse for the Union army. After the war, she settled in New York State and became a leader in the struggle for women's rights.

Harriet Tubman

Index